COOL CHEMICALS!

The Chemistry of **Technology**

Written by Joseph P. Cataliotti

WORLD BOOK

www.worldbook.com

Co-published by agreement between Shi Tu Hui and World Book, Inc.

Shi Tu Hui
Room 1807, Block 1,
#3 West Dawang Road
Chaoyang District, Beijing 100025
P.R. China

World Book, Inc.
180 North LaSalle Street
Suite 900
Chicago, Illinois 60601
USA

© 2026. All rights reserved. This volume may not be reproduced in whole or in part in any form without prior written permission from the publisher.

WORLD BOOK and the GLOBE DEVICE are registered trademarks or trademarks of World Book, Inc.

Library of Congress Control Number: 2025942240

Aha! Academy: Chemistry
ISBN: 978-0-7166-7346-0 (set, hardcover)

Cool Chemicals! The Chemistry of Technology
ISBN: 978-0-7166-7353-8 (hard cover)
ISBN: 978-0-7166-7373-6 (e-book)
ISBN: 978-0-7166-7363-7 (soft cover)

Staff

Editorial

Vice President
Tom Evans

Senior Manager, New Content
Jeff De La Rosa

Associate Manager, New Content
William D. Adams

Senior Curriculum Designer
Caroline Davidson

Curriculum Designer
Mikayla Kightlinger

Proofreader
Nathalie Strassheim

Indexer
Nathaniel Lindstrom

Graphics and Design

Senior Visual
Communications Designer
Melanie Bender

Designer
Shannon Hagman

Written by Joseph P. Cataliotti

Designed by Starletta Polster

Acknowledgments

The publishers gratefully acknowledge the following sources for photography. All illustrations were prepared by WORLD BOOK unless otherwise noted.

Cover: Elena11/Shutterstock; IM Imagery/Shutterstock; Thx4Stock team/Shutterstock; Quality Stock Arts/Shutterstock; ViDI Studio/Shutterstock

dokola (licensed under CC0 1.0) 4; Jynto (licensed under CC0 1.0) 11; © Piemags/POND5 10; Public Domain 7; Public Domain (NASA) 11; © Shutterstock 3, 4, 5, 6, 7, 8, 9, 10, 11, 12, 13, 14, 15, 16, 17, 18, 19, 20, 21, 22, 23, 24, 25, 26, 27, 28, 29, 30, 31, 32, 33, 34, 35, 36, 37, 38, 39, 40, 41, 42, 43, 44, 45, 46, 47, 48; Wellcome Library (licensed under CC BY 4.0) 15; © WORLD BOOK diagram by Jay Bensen

There is a glossary of terms on page 48. Terms defined in the glossary are in type that looks like *this* on their first appearance on any spread (two facing pages).

Contents

Introduction	4
① **Cool materials**	**6**
Nanotechnology	8
Carbon nanotubes	10
Quantum dots	12
② **Battery power**	**14**
Battery science	16
Vital element: lithium	18
Lithium-ion batteries	20
Solid-state batteries	22
Rust batteries?	24
③ **Semiconductors**	**26**
Semiconductor science	28
Vital element: silicon	30
Swapping silicon	32
④ **Earth-saving chemistry**	**34**
Power from the sun	36
Perovskite crystals	38
Splitting water	40
Reusing & recycling plastic	42
Split water molecules	44
Index	46
Glossary	48

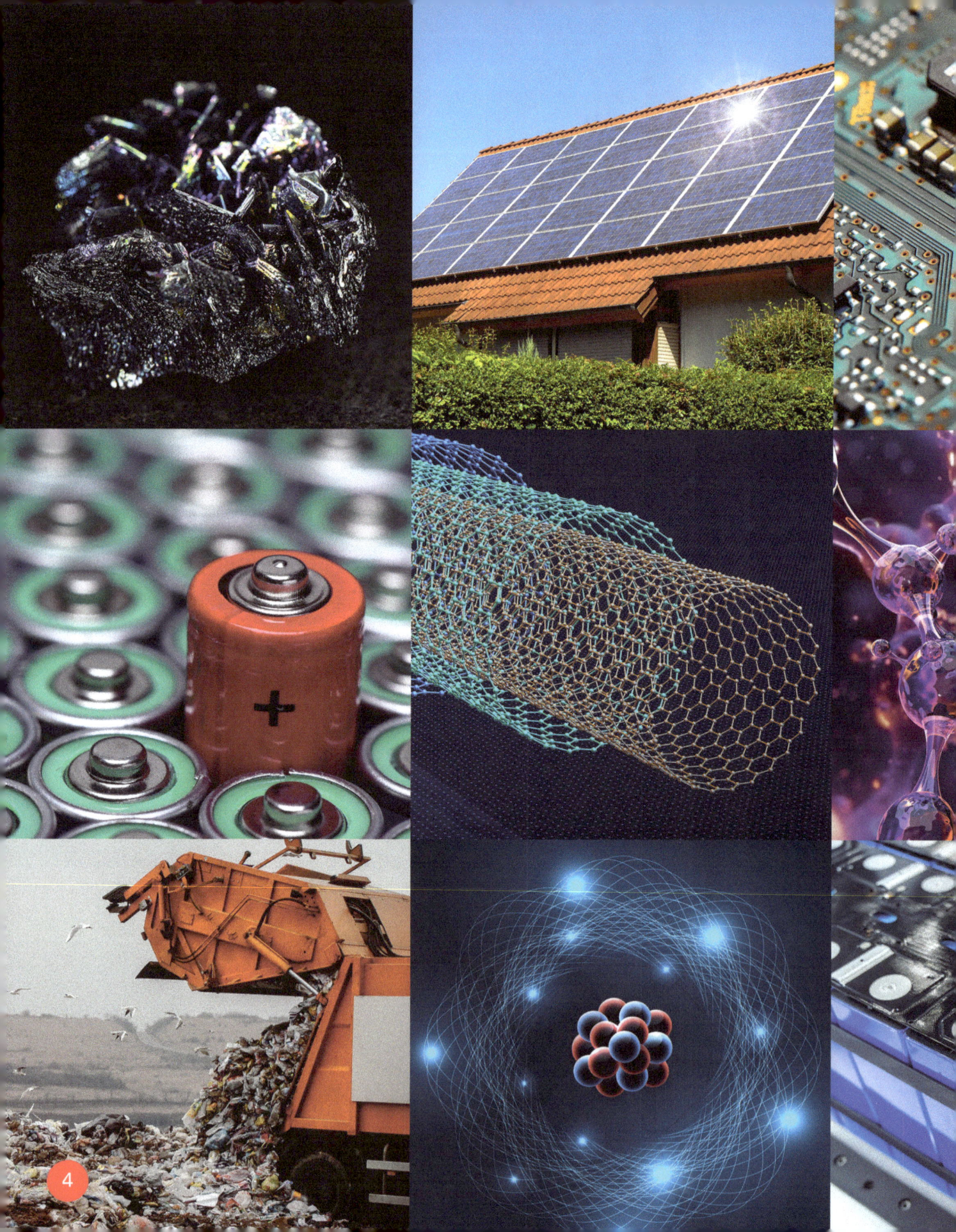

Introduction

Technology is so cool! It enables you to immerse yourself in a video game, fly a drone, or watch any movie you want.

Technology is also advancing at an astounding rate. Go ask your parents! They may remember a time when a pocket-sized device that could make video calls and access almost all the information in the world seemed like science fiction!

At the heart of all this technology is chemistry—the study of the substances that make up everything and how they interact. Through chemistry, scientists can make panels that harness the power of the sun, microscopic machines, and powerful batteries.

Read on to learn about the chemistry of technology!

I'm positive you'll enjoy reading this!

1 COOL MATERIALS

If you zoom in very, very close to this book, you would see trillions upon trillions of tiny *atoms*. The properties and interactions of these atoms are key to technology.

But what exactly are atoms?

The atom is the basic unit of matter. Everything around us is made up of different types of atoms. Even the largest atom is impossibly tiny!

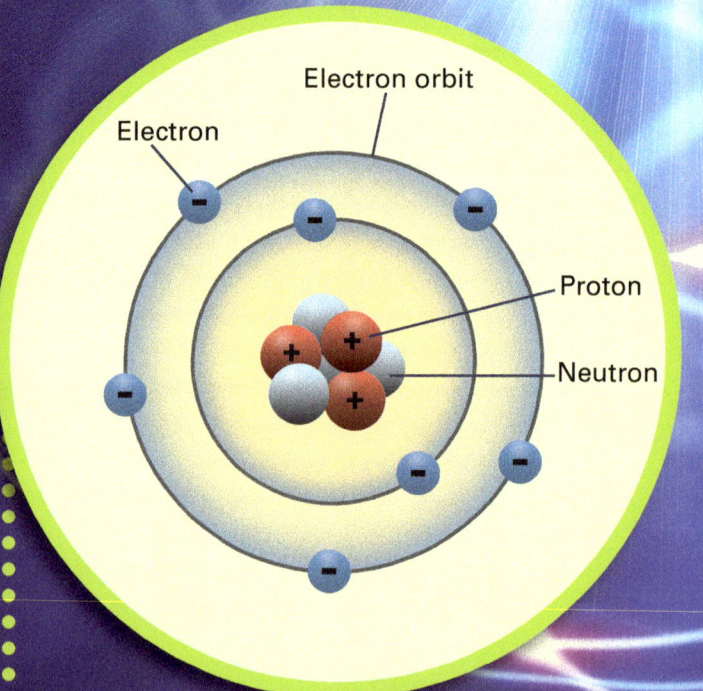

Electron orbit
Electron
Proton
Neutron

Inside an atom are three different types of even smaller particles.
In the nucleus (center) of an atom are protons and neutrons. Buzzing around the nucleus are *electrons*. Protons have a positive charge, and electrons a negative charge.

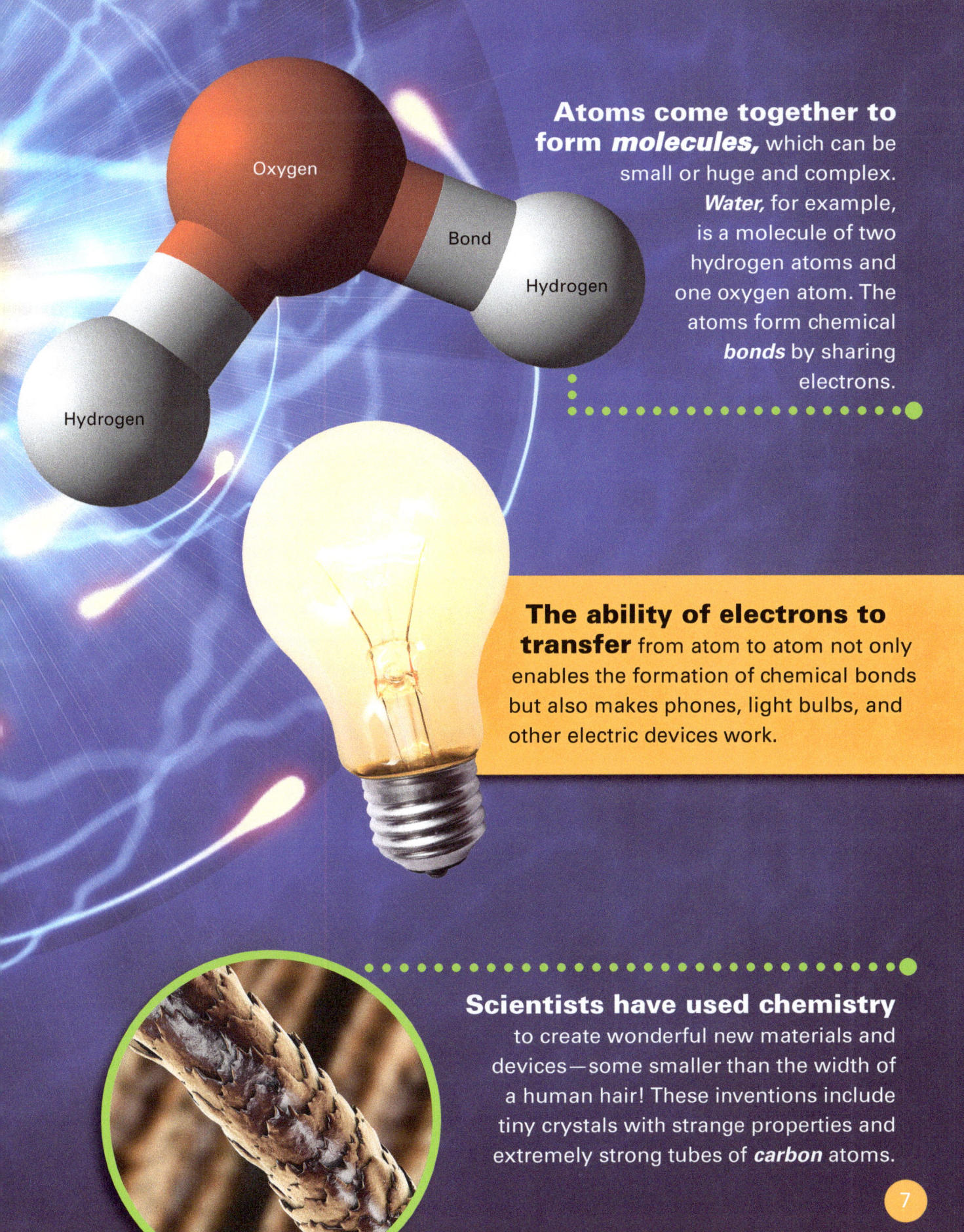

Atoms come together to form *molecules*, which can be small or huge and complex. *Water,* for example, is a molecule of two hydrogen atoms and one oxygen atom. The atoms form chemical *bonds* by sharing electrons.

The ability of electrons to transfer from atom to atom not only enables the formation of chemical bonds but also makes phones, light bulbs, and other electric devices work.

Scientists have used chemistry to create wonderful new materials and devices—some smaller than the width of a human hair! These inventions include tiny crystals with strange properties and extremely strong tubes of *carbon* atoms.

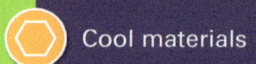

Cool materials

Nanotechnology

What is nanotechnology, anyway? Nanotechnology is the creation and study of structures that are slightly larger than atoms and molecules. It involves working on the nanometer scale, or nanoscale. Nano means billionth. A nanometer is 0.000000001 meter ($\frac{1}{25,400,000}$ inch)!

1 nanometer = 0.000000001 meter

Scientists can arrange *atoms* into tiny, orderly ***crystals*** called nanocrystals. Nanocrystals can have unusual properties. For example, certain types of nanocrystals emit light when they absorb energy. The color of the light depends on the crystal's size and shape.

TECH TIME

Scientists make nanoscale structures using different techniques. One method, called ***electron*** beam lithography, uses a beam of electrons to etch a mass of material into a shape. In another method, sensitive probes manipulate individual atoms or ***molecules***.

Through the power of science, we can create and study tiny molecular structures smaller than one-thousandth the width of a human hair! This field of research is called nanotechnology.

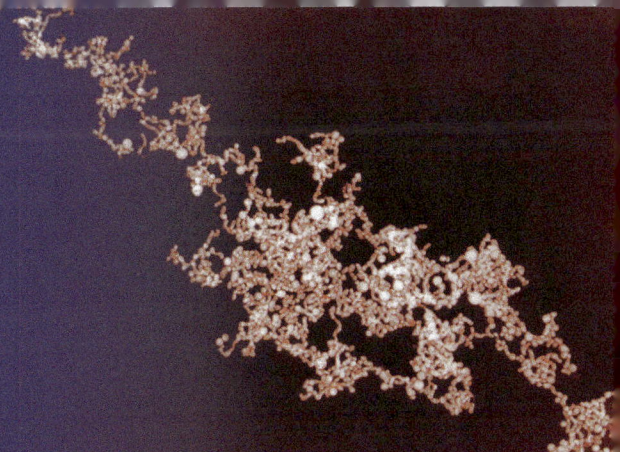

Why is nanotechnology so important? Nanoscale materials, and the objects made from them, can display fundamentally different properties and behavior than the similar materials at larger scales.

By combining nanoparticles or other nanoscale objects with such conventional materials as metal, plastic, or ceramic, scientists make nanocomposites. Nanocomposites can be stronger, lighter, and longer-lasting than conventional materials. For example, car exteriors made with plastic nanocomposites may be more resistant to scratches and dents.

Scientists can also create tiny machines made up of atoms—nanodevices. For example, some scientists are developing "smart dust," nanoscale sensors that can disperse through the air much like regular household dust.

Cool materials

Carbon nanotubes

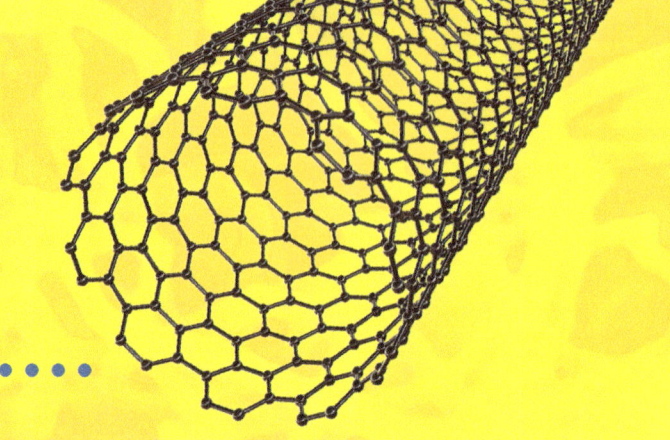

- **Nanotubes are tube-shaped structures of carbon atoms** several nanometers in diameter and several thousand nanometers in length. All the carbon atoms are connected by *bonds,* so each nanotube is actually a single giant *molecule* of carbon!

Due to their robust atomic structure, nanotubes are about 100 times stronger than steel. Some can even conduct an electric *current,* too!

Strong and lightweight, nanotubes have many applications in spacecraft. They can be used in lightweight cables, insulation, and shielding against dangerous radiation.

One key nanotechnology is the *carbon* nanotube—a tiny tube-shaped structure made of carbon *atoms*. Despite nanotubes' tiny size, they're very tough!

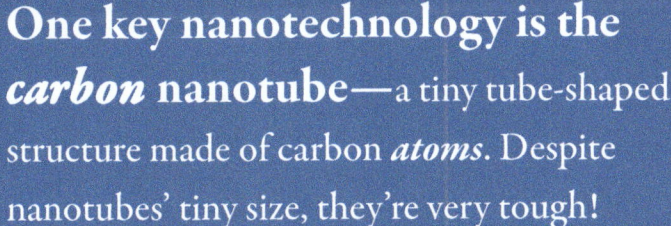

Carbon nanotubes are one of many different carbon structures called fullerenes.

They aren't just found in laboratories! Small amounts of fullerenes occur naturally in rock and in sooty flames, such as those of candles. They have also been detected near old stars.

Buckminsterfullerenes, also known as buckyballs, are spheres of bonded carbon atoms. They look like tiny soccer balls!

CURIOUS CONNECTIONS

Buckyballs are being studied for use in medicine. Some scientists are working to encapsulate drugs inside these tough carbon cages, protecting them for safe delivery to specific parts of the body.

Cool materials

Quantum dots

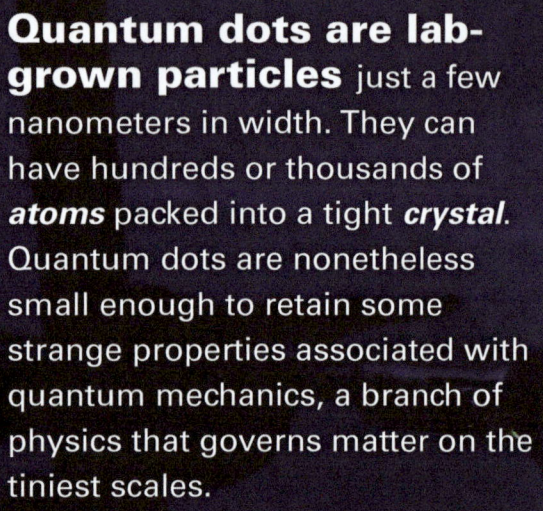

Quantum dots are lab-grown particles just a few nanometers in width. They can have hundreds or thousands of *atoms* packed into a tight *crystal*. Quantum dots are nonetheless small enough to retain some strange properties associated with quantum mechanics, a branch of physics that governs matter on the tiniest scales.

CAREER CORNER

Quantum dots are at the cutting edge of science. If you study and work hard, you too can help develop new materials as a physical chemist.

Quantum dots are tiny particles with special properties. They may seem magical, but chemistry and physics can explain their wonders.

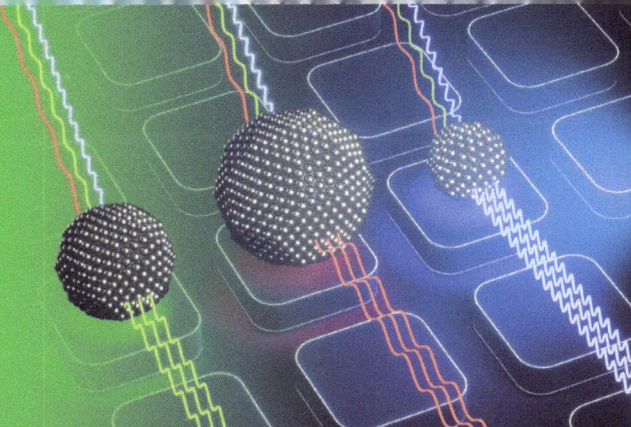

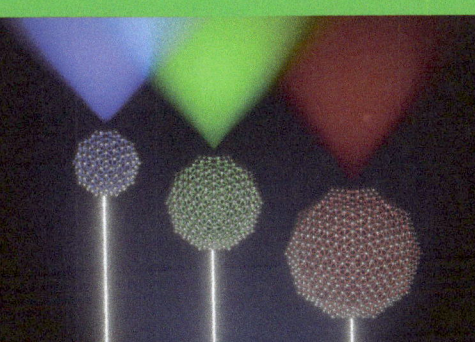

When ultraviolet light shines on quantum dots, they glow different colors, depending on their size. This effect occurs because light waves excite quantum dots' *electrons*, causing them to emit their own light. Larger dots glow red, and smaller dots glow green or blue.

This glowing property makes quantum dots useful in many different applications. Scientists can use them, for example, to illuminate different parts of cells. They can also be used to create tiny displays, just like the pixels in your television!

Cadmium sulfide

Scientists make quantum dots from semiconductors, such as cadmium sulfide or cadmium selenide, which can conduct electricity. They inject these compounds into a very hot liquid, forming crystals. The crystals vary in size depending on how long they're cooked. Scientists can make different color dots in this way!

2
BATTERY POWER

Batteries power plenty of the neat technology you use every day. But how exactly do batteries work?

Electrons—those tiny particles that buzz around *atoms*—are the key to understanding batteries. Batteries work by being plugged into a circuit—a looping path, usually made of metal wire. Batteries can separate the negatively charged electrons from an atom and "push" them through the circuit. The flow of electrons through the circuit forms a *current*.

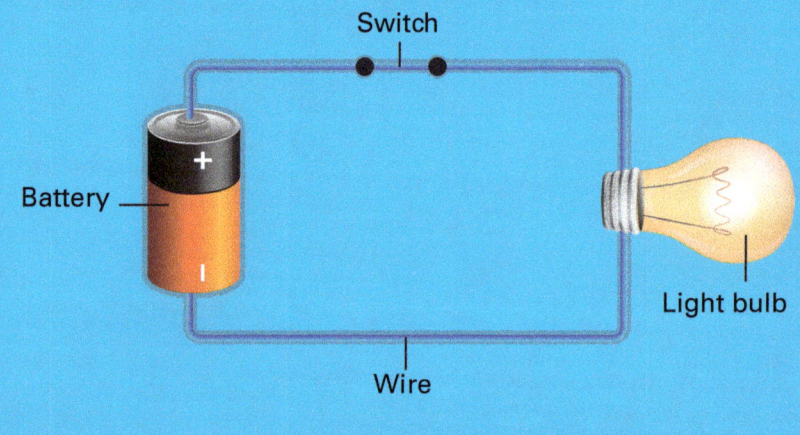

Switch • Battery • Light bulb • Wire

Then what? Well, if you connect some sort of device to the circuit, that device can convert the electric current's energy into other useful forms of energy, such as light, sound, and motion. The device can be as simple as a light bulb or as complex as a modern smartphone!

There are many different types of batteries. One type of battery that is growing more and more important is the **lithium-ion** battery, which makes use of the chemical element lithium.

I get a charge out of chemistry!

One of the first batteries, called the voltaic pile, was invented around 1800 by the Italian scientist **Alessandro Volta.** The voltaic pile consisted of layers of metal plates separated by cardboard or a woven cloth soaked in solution. The *volt,* a unit of electrical measurement, is named in honor of Volta.

 Battery power

Battery science

Batteries have two basic parts: an anode, marked with a minus sign (−), and a cathode, marked with a plus sign (+). Different types of batteries have anodes and cathodes of different materials, but the principles are the same—chemical *reactions* at the anode and cathode provide the energy to "push" *electrons* around the circuit, creating a *current*.

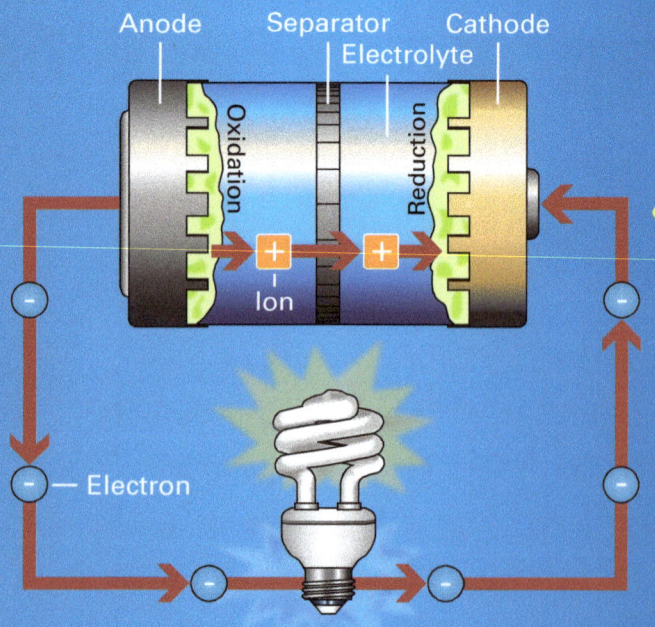

In a chemical reaction, the *atoms* that form a *molecule* either *bond* with new atoms or split apart. Chemical reactions are at the heart of chemistry.

Oxidation reactions take place at the anode. Atoms lose electrons, and these electrons are "pushed" around the circuit. Reduction reactions take place at the cathode. These atoms gain electrons pushed around the circuit. Different specific reactions take place in different types of batteries, but the basics are the same. At their heart is chemistry!

What do *batteries* have to do with chemistry?

Batteries get their electrical energy from chemical energy.

There are two main types of batteries: primary batteries, which can't be recharged, and secondary batteries, which can be recharged. *Lithium-ion* batteries, for example, are secondary batteries.

DID YOU KNOW?

Regular consumer batteries are made of various substances, including zinc (the anode) and manganese dioxide (the cathode).

Manganese dioxide

Zinc

Vital element: lithium

STATS

Symbol
Li

Atomic Number
3

Atomic Mass
6.941

Melting Point
365.97 °F (180.54 °C)

Boiling Point
2457 °F (1347 °C)

Discoverer
Johann Arfvedson

Lithium is a soft, silvery-white metallic element. It can be found in the rechargeable *batteries* used in new technologies. Electric cars, electric scooters, laptop computers, cell phones, and power tools often use lithium-ion batteries.

Each lithium *atom* has three protons in its nucleus (core). Each of those protons attracts an *electron*. Two of the electrons, however, elbow away the third from the positively charged nucleus. This outer electron can be easily drawn away by other molecules or atoms. This makes lithium especially reactive.

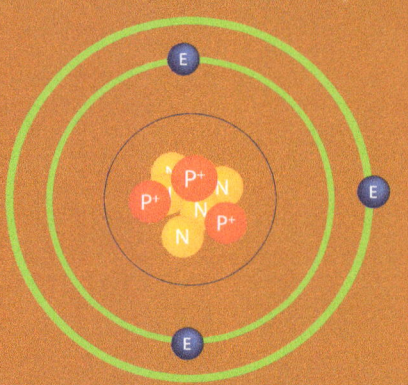

***Lithium* is the lightest metal.** Its unique chemical properties are the reason so many new technologies rely on lithium.

Pure lithium isn't commonly found in nature because it combines easily with other elements. For example, it reacts with **water** to release hydrogen gas.

← Lithium fields

Lithium compounds are used in the manufacture of various materials, including ceramic products, enamels, glass, and lubricants for use at high temperatures. They are also used in rubber products and in dyes for textiles.

CURIOUS CONNECTIONS

PSYCHIATRY One lithium compound, lithium carbonate, is used as a drug to treat bipolar disorder.

Battery power

Lithium-ion batteries

Lithium-ion batteries store energy more efficiently and last longer than other common kinds of batteries. Plus, they're rechargeable. What a bodacious battery!

When an *atom* gains or loses an *electron,* it gains an electric charge. Scientists call such an atom an ion. Ions are attracted to other ions of opposite charge.

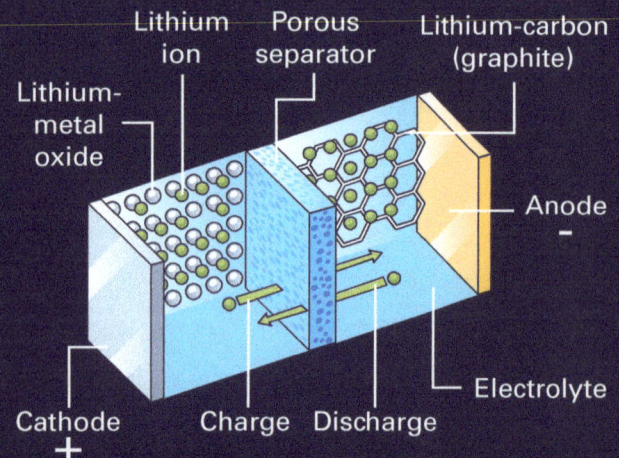

Something special happens inside a lithium-ion battery when it produces an electric *current*. Each lithium atom loses an electron to become an ion. It then moves from the anode to the cathode through a fluid called the electrolyte.

One particular type of *battery* is at the heart of many electronic devices you might know or use—the powerful, rechargeable *lithium* battery.

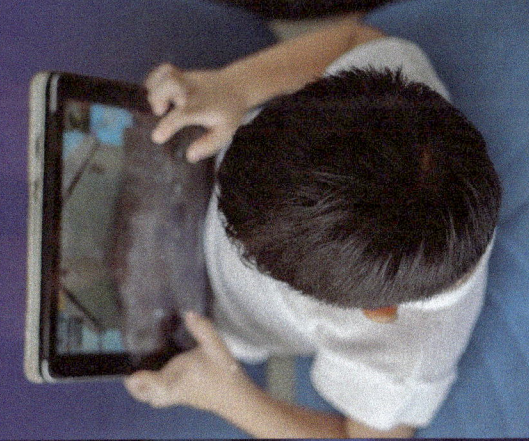

This chemical *reaction* can be reversed by running a stronger current through the battery. The lithium ions return to the anode with their lost electrons, recharging the battery. Afterward, the battery can again convert chemical energy into electric energy again.

So, lithium-ion batteries work via stable, reversible reactions. Not only that, but they're more powerful than other rechargeable batteries. What's not to love?

In the late 1900's and early 2000's, manufacturers began developing **large lithium-ion batteries** that could power electric vehicle motors. Vroom!

21

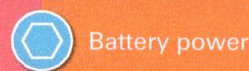
Battery power

Solid-state batteries

Regular lithium batteries contain a liquid electrolyte. Lithium ions move through the electrolyte from the anode to the cathode and back again. Solid-state lithium batteries, as the name suggests, have a solid electrolyte.

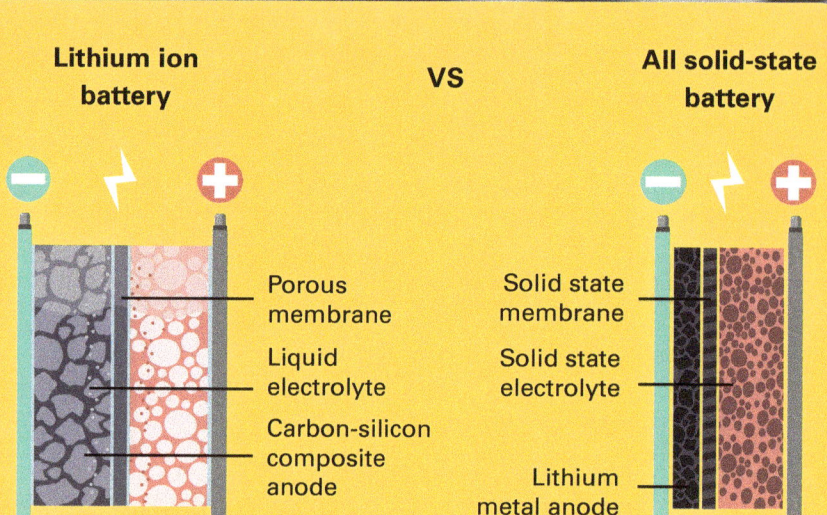

Lithium ion battery VS All solid-state battery
- Porous membrane
- Liquid electrolyte
- Carbon-silicon composite anode
- Solid state membrane
- Solid state electrolyte
- Lithium metal anode

In solid-state batteries, the lithium **atoms** still travel back and forth between the anode and cathode to produce energy. So, when the battery is being used, lithium metal builds up on the cathode. It is stripped away when the battery is charged.

Why are solid-state lithium batteries so promising? Regular lithium batteries have several drawbacks. For example, they can build up excess heat and even catch fire. Solid-state batteries cannot overheat this way and therefore are much safer.

Solid-state *batteries* are on the cutting edge of science. They have several advantages over regular *lithium* batteries, but several weaknesses as well.

Solid-state batteries can have other advantages as well. Lithium metal solid-state batteries can be lighter than regular lithium batteries, for example, improving the efficiency of electric vehicles.

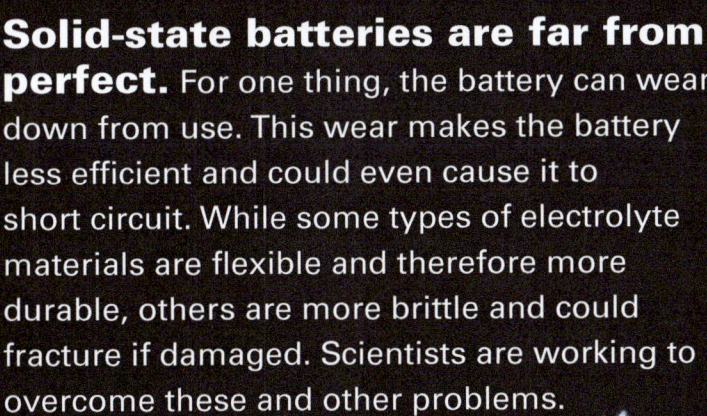

Solid-state batteries are far from perfect. For one thing, the battery can wear down from use. This wear makes the battery less efficient and could even cause it to short circuit. While some types of electrolyte materials are flexible and therefore more durable, others are more brittle and could fracture if damaged. Scientists are working to overcome these and other problems.

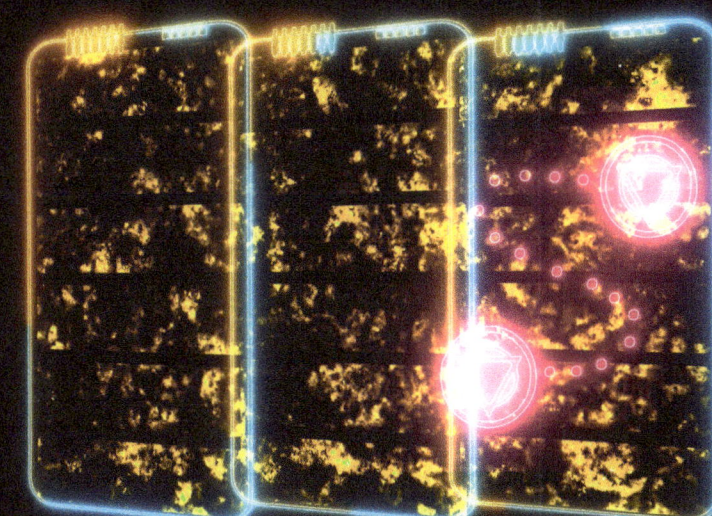

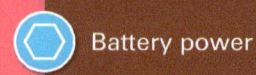
Battery power

Rust batteries?

One problem with renewable energy sources, such as solar and wind, is that sometimes the sun does not shine and the wind does not blow. For renewable sources of electricity to meet demand, they must rely on batteries to store energy. However, regular large batteries aren't able to efficiently store electricity for many hours.

We tend to think of rust as a bad thing. But rust-powered *batteries* made of iron may provide a key to future renewable energy.

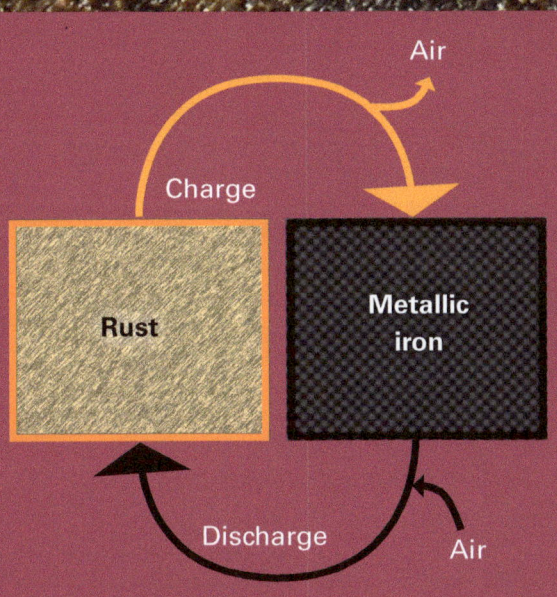

Iron-air batteries may be able to help. The key chemical mechanism in iron-air batteries is...rusting! On either side of the electrolyte in an iron-air battery are an air cathode and an iron anode. As iron-air batteries generate electricity, hydroxide (OH⁻) ions travel through the electrolyte to the anode to form rust. That's right, entire *molecules* can be ions, too! When iron-air batteries are charged, that rust is split apart back into iron and hydroxide.

Iron-air batteries were first devised in the late 1960's by the United States National Aeronautics and Space Administration (NASA). However, it is only recently that advances in battery technology have made them an intriguing option.

3
SEMI-CONDUCTORS

Semiconductors are in everything these days: phones, laptops, cars, and even high-end toasters! A computer chip is a piece of a semiconductor, usually *silicon,* that contains an electronic circuit. Solar panels are made of semiconductor materials, too.

What exactly are semiconductors, though?

Conductors, such as copper wire, carry electric *current* very well. Such insulators as glass don't conduct current well at all. Semiconductors are somewhere in the middle. Unlike an insulator, a semiconductor will conduct a small electric current at room temperature. And unlike a metal, a semiconductor will conduct more current as its temperature is increased. These characteristics are a result of the semiconductor's atoms and the *crystals* they form.

Modern computers would be impossible without *semiconductors*. It's only through science that we can understand and use these strange materials.

DID YOU KNOW?

LED light bulbs contain a semiconductor. When electrons flow through it, the bulb glows!

Silicon (Si) is the most widely used semiconductor. By adding other elements to a silicon semiconductor, scientists can improve its conductivity. Other major semiconductors include germanium (Ge) and gallium arsenide (GaAs).

Silicon (Si)

Germanium (Ge)

Semiconductors

Semiconductor science

Semiconductors conduct electricity worse than such metals as copper but better than such insulators as glass. The chemical properties of semiconductor materials explain why this is the case.

Silicon is a semiconductor material. Each *atom* of the element silicon has 14 protons, so it attracts 14 *electrons*. If a silicon atom has 14 electrons, it is electrically neutral.

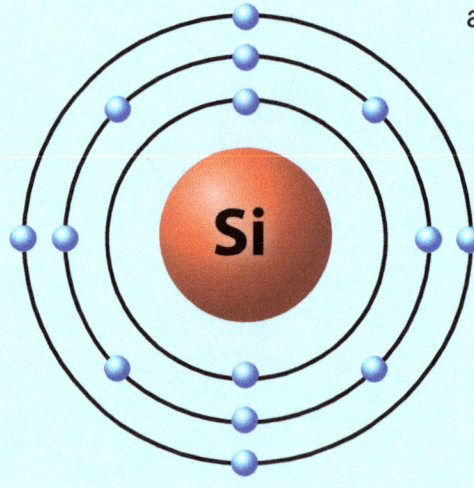

The electrons of a silicon atom are arranged in three shells around the nucleus (core) of the atom. The innermost shell has two electrons, the middle shell has eight, and the outermost shell has four. Silicon atoms can *bond* together to form large orderly *molecules* called *crystals*. To form these bonds, the atoms share their outer electrons with their neighbors.

Scientists use *semiconductors* because of their unique properties. Electrons, as usual, play a key role.

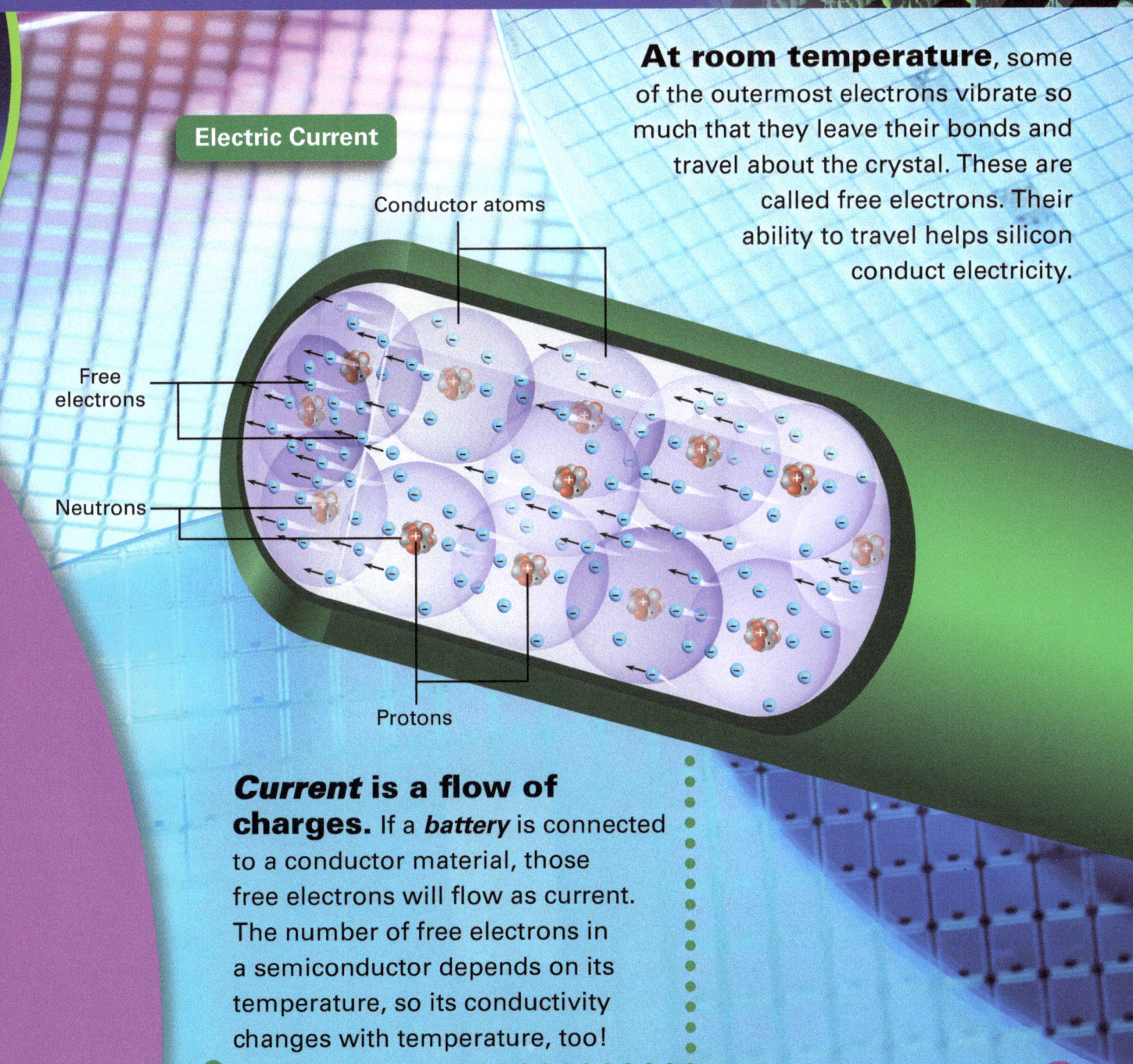

Electric Current

Conductor atoms

Free electrons

Neutrons

Protons

At room temperature, some of the outermost electrons vibrate so much that they leave their bonds and travel about the crystal. These are called free electrons. Their ability to travel helps silicon conduct electricity.

***Current* is a flow of charges.** If a *battery* is connected to a conductor material, those free electrons will flow as current. The number of free electrons in a semiconductor depends on its temperature, so its conductivity changes with temperature, too!

Semiconductors

Vital element: silicon

oxygen silicon oxygen

SiO₂

STATS

Symbol
Si

Atomic Number
14

Atomic Mass
28.0855

Melting point
2570 °F (1410 °C)

Boiling point
4271 °F (2355 °C)

Discoverer
Jöns Berzelius

Silicon is a hard, dark gray metalloid that has a shiny luster. In nature, silicon occurs primarily in silicon dioxide (SiO_2), also known as silica, and in compounds known as silicates. A silicate contains units of one silicon *atom* and four oxygen atoms (SiO_4) along with one or more metallic elements.

SiO_2 is the main ingredient of sand, quartz, agate, and glass. It is used in optical fibers, ceramic products, and the quartz *crystals* in electronic devices. Many rocks are made up of silicate minerals.

Silicon is a critical element in technology.

Silicon Valley, a global center for technological innovation in California, gets its name from this element.

Silicates are the principal building material the world over in the form of cut stone, bricks, and concrete. Many gemstones are SiO_2 or SiO_4 minerals.

Silicon carbide (SiC), also known by the trade name Carborundum, is a compound with *carbon* that ranks as one of the hardest materials known. Manufacturers use it to grind and polish other materials.

Silicones are synthetic compounds with carbon and oxygen. They are used in synthetic rubber, *water* repellent coatings, nonstick surfaces, lubricants, electrical insulators, and sealants.

DID YOU KNOW?

Silicon makes up about 28 percent of Earth's crust. Only oxygen is more plentiful.

And of course, silicon is the main substance in computer chips, solar cells, transistors, and other electronic devices.

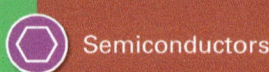 Semiconductors

Swapping silicon

Scientists use a process called doping to make silicon crystals more conductive. Silicon crystals are made up of many silicon *atoms* sharing *bonds*. In the interior of the crystal, the four outer electrons of the silicon atoms tend to be stuck in bonds, limiting the crystal's conductivity. Swapping out small amounts of silicon atoms with other atoms, however, can help free up electrons to move, making the crystal more conductive.

TECH TIME

By combining n-doping and p-doping, scientists can use semiconductors for all sorts of advanced but beneficial technologies.

Silicon crystals are a basic semiconductor material. However, silicon crystals can be made more conductive through chemistry.

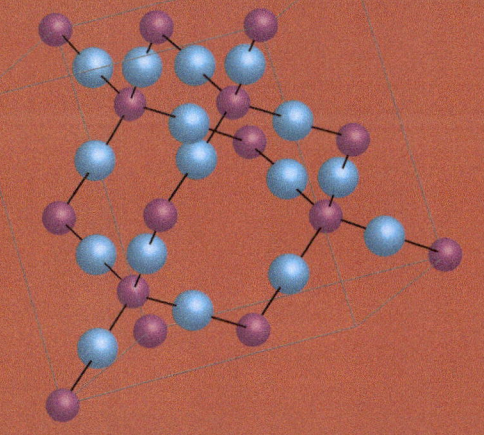

There are two types of doping:

N-doping

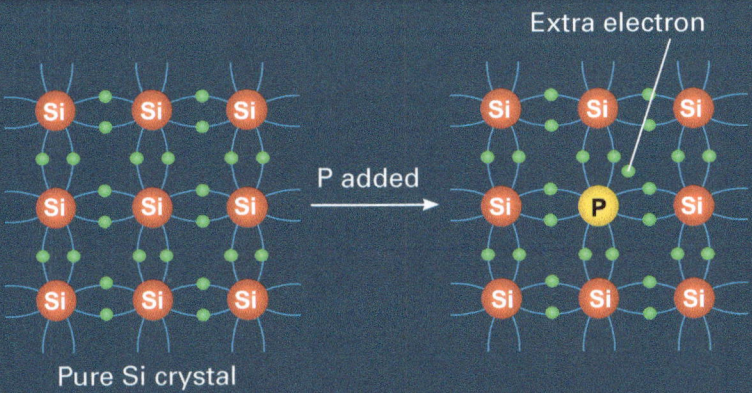

Pure Si crystal → P added → Extra electron

A crystal can be n-doped by swapping some of its silicon atoms with an element with five outer electrons, such as phosphorus (P). That extra electron, not stuck in any bonds, can zip about as a free electron. The "n" stand for its charge: negative.

Phosphorus

P-doping

A crystal can be p-doped by swapping some silicon atoms with an element with three outer electrons, such as boron (B). This leaves a "hole" in the crystal's electron configuration for electrons to move into. The "p" refers to the hole's positive charge.

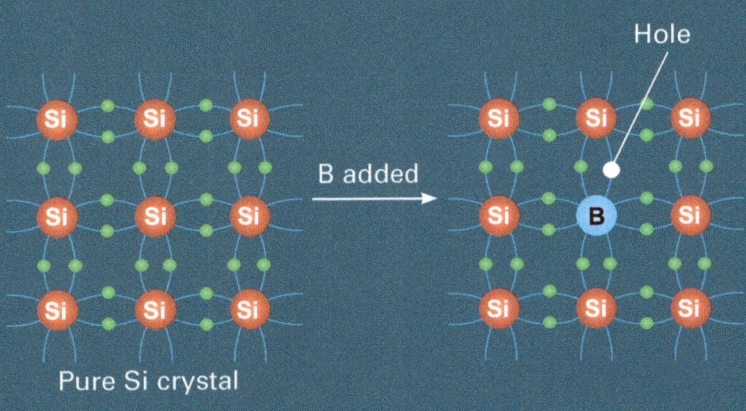

Pure Si crystal → B added → Hole

Boron

4 EARTH-SAVING CHEMISTRY

Over the past centuries, human activities have polluted our environment and released a huge quantity of greenhouse gases from burned fossil fuels into the atmosphere. Greenhouse gases trap heat from sunlight, causing climate change. New technologies may help us confront this global problem.

Solar energy is a leading alternative to fossil fuels. Solar panels use semiconductor materials to convert sunlight into electricity. Most use silicon, but the mineral perovskite may prove to be a better alternative.

Hydrogen is another promising alternative to fossil fuels. Scientists are developing ways to make hydrogen from water in a process called photocatalysis.

Climate change is one of the world's most pressing issues, but emerging technologies might help us fight it.

Plastic pollution has also become a major environmental problem. New chemical recycling methods could help. Together, these technologies could play a key role in combating climate change and reducing humanity's environmental impact.

Modern climate change can be traced to the **Industrial Revolution,** when human beings first began to burn large quantities of fossil fuels to power factories.

Earth-saving chemistry

Power from the sun

Solar panels, also known as photovoltaic cells or solar cells, produce electricity from sunlight using semiconductor materials.

CURIOUS CONNECTIONS

ELECTRICAL ENGINEERING

You can do more than just produce power from sunlight with these materials. The transistor uses thin layers of doped semiconductors to make switches without any moving parts! Transistors are a key part of almost every kind of electronic device.

Solar panels provide clean and abundant power. Switching to solar energy can help the world combat climate change.

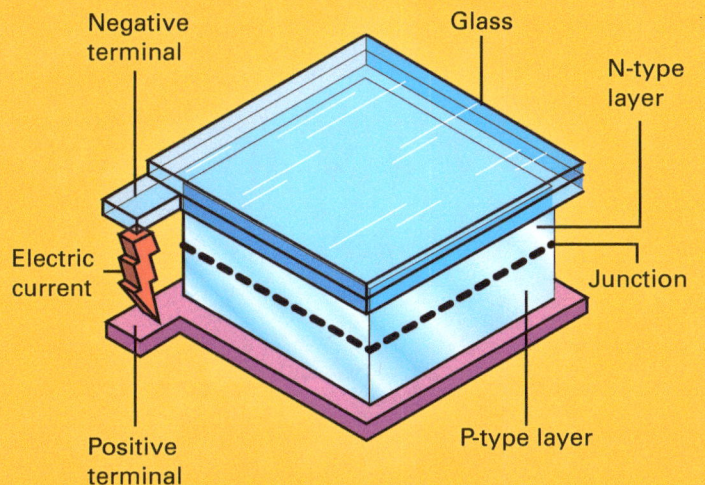

Solar cells work by combining p-doped and n-doped semiconductors. When the two are sandwiched together, an n-doped semiconductor's free electrons move to neighboring areas of a p-doped semiconductor. The p-doped border region becomes negatively charged with these extra electrons, and the n-doped border region becomes positively charged due to a lack of electrons. This border region, called the depletion layer, blocks more electrons from hopping across. So, the **current** is blocked.

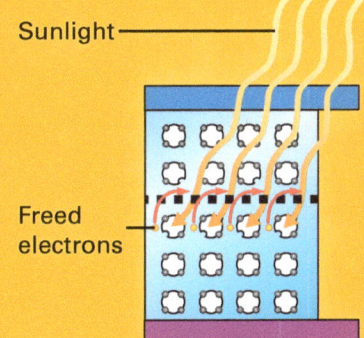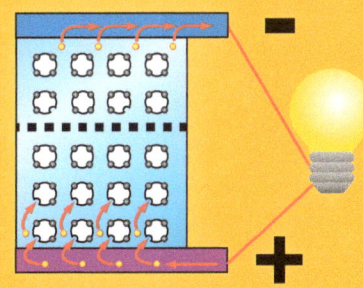

Sunlight can excite the electrons, enabling more and more of them to jump from the p-doped semiconductor into the already negatively charged n-doped semiconductor. The result is a build up of electrons in one layer and a major lack of electrons in the other. Connecting these regions with a conductive wire enables the buildup of electrons to flow, creating an electric current. This process is called the photovoltaic effect.

Earth-saving chemistry

Perovskite crystals

Perovskite is a mineral made of *crystals* of calcium, titanium, and oxygen with a distinctive lattice shape. The name perovskite is also applied to other materials with a similar crystal structure.

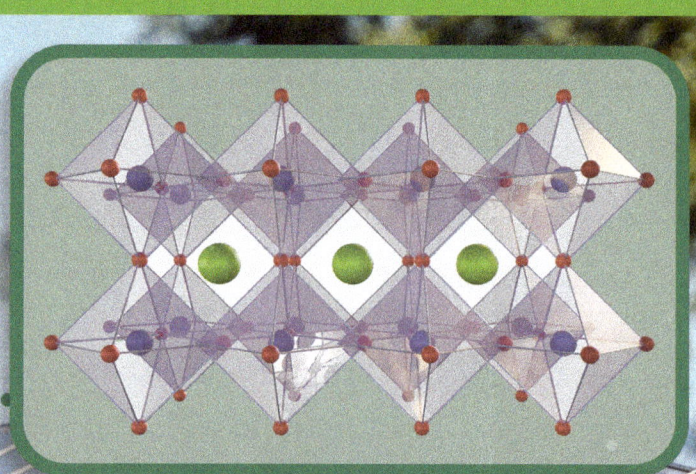

Perovskite solar cells

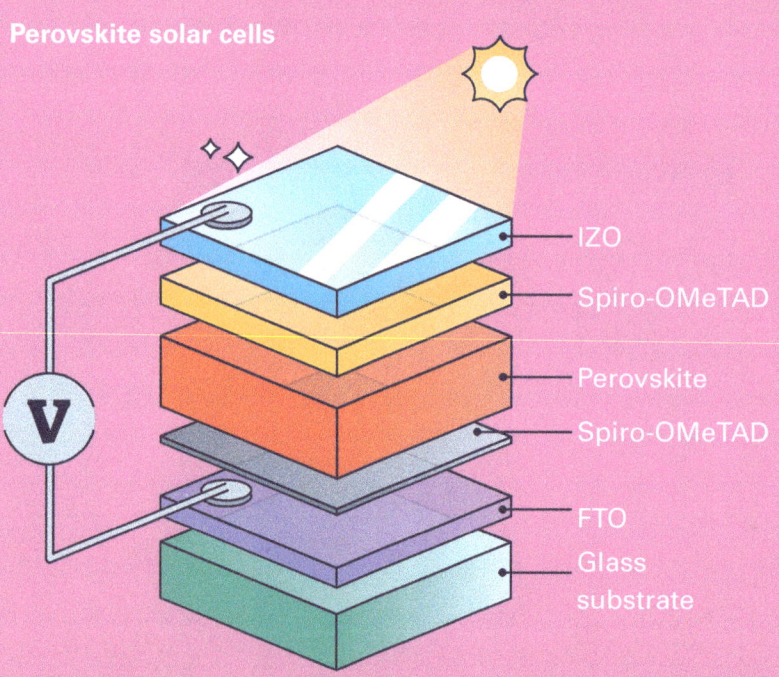

IZO
Spiro-OMeTAD
Perovskite
Spiro-OMeTAD
FTO
Glass substrate

Perovskites may be an excellent alternative to *silicon* in solar panels. The silicon used in solar panels must be very pure, and solar panels are therefore expensive to make. But perovskite is cheap! In addition, perovskite solar panels convert sunlight to electricity more efficiently than silicon. They're also lighter than traditional solar panels—a trio of advantages!

Solar panel technology can be improved upon. The mineral perovskite could be used to make the next generation of sunlight harvesters!

If perovskite solar panels are so great, why aren't we using them now? Perovskite solar panels are not very durable. Exposure to rain and extended sunlight or heating can damage them. Solar panels, as you can guess, have to weather rain, sunlight, and heat!

Scientists are studying new ways to increase the durability of perovskite solar panels. In recent years, they have learned that using a protective layer of transparent material, such as glass or plastic, can prevent the panels from losing efficiency due to environmental damage. Adding nickel oxide or other substances to the semiconductor can also stabilize a perovskite panel's electricity output. Much more work remains for future experiments!

⬢ Earth-saving chemistry

Splitting water

Experts have suggested replacing such fossil fuels as coal, oil, and natural gas with more widespread use of hydrogen. Hydrogen could be a renewable fuel that produces little pollution. Devices called fuel cells can produce electrical energy by reacting hydrogen with oxygen to make *water*.

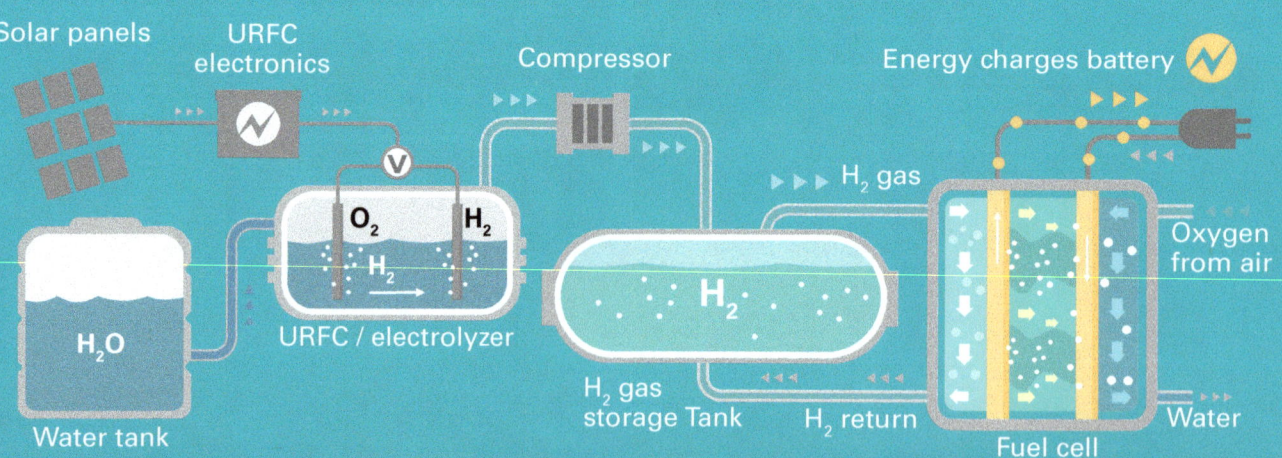

GreenHydrogen Fuel Cell Energy

Solar panels — URFC electronics — Compressor — Energy charges battery

Water tank (H_2O) — URFC / electrolyzer (O_2, H_2) — H_2 gas storage Tank — H_2 return — Fuel cell — Oxygen from air — Water — H_2 gas

Producing H_2 requires energy, however, which tends to be obtained by burning fossil fuels. To reduce fossil fuel consumption, engineers must develop efficient ways to make H_2. One way is by splitting water (H_2O) using sunlight.

Climate change from greenhouse gas emissions is a serious challenge for the world. Hydrogen (H_2) fuel may provide an answer.

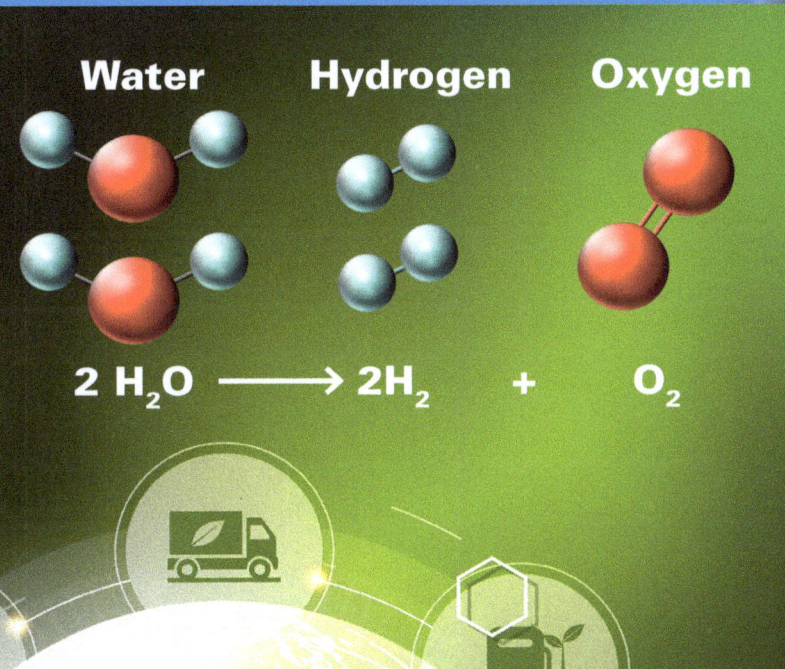

$$2\,H_2O \longrightarrow 2H_2 + O_2$$

One way to split water is through photocatalysis. In this multistep process, a beam of sunlight excites the *electrons* of water *molecules* and a nearby *semiconductor*. At an anode, each water molecule loses two electrons and splits apart. These hydrogen *atoms* don't *bond* together yet, however. At the cathode, two electrons join two hydrogen atoms to bond them into H_2. This process is helped by other molecules called photocatalysts.

Photocatalytic production of hydrogen is a promising technology, but it has not been widely adopted due to issues with efficiency.

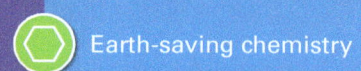

Earth-saving chemistry

Reusing & recycling plastic

Plastics are very useful. Humans make hundreds of millions of metric tons of plastic every year!

Plastic is made of long chains of *molecules* called polymers. Polymers are prized for their durability, but that creates a double-edged sword—most plastics take a long time to decompose (break down).

Once we're done with plastic, most of it is either dumped in gigantic landfills, tossed as litter, or burned. Plastic pollution is a major issue, with plastic waste found everywhere across the planet. Only about 10 percent of plastic is recycled, because recycling most plastic is difficult and expensive.

Plastics are a major source of pollution across the world. Chemical recycling may provide a solution to this problem!

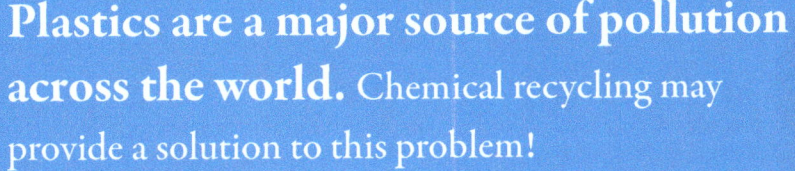

Scientists, however, are devising new methods to recycle plastic through the power of chemistry. In one process, called pyrolysis, plastic waste is superheated to break it down into a liquid sludge called pyrolysis oil. Scientists can then use a complicated chemical *reaction* to create aldehydes, which can be used to create other industrial chemicals. In another method, the plastic oil is refined and gasified at even hotter temperatures to make a type of fuel. Besides fuel and industrial chemicals, plastic that has gone through these processes can even be made again into plastic ready for consumers.

CAREER CORNER

Are you interested in using science to confront climate change and polluton? You can become an environmental scientist!

43

Split water molecules

What you'll need:
- A 9-volt battery
- Water
- A transparent cup
- Two wooden graphite pencils
- A pencil sharpener
- A small piece of cardboard or paper

Give it a try
1. Pour water into the transparent cup.
2. Remove the wooden pencils' erasers, if they have them, and sharpen the pencils on either end, so that they have two tips.
3. Place the paper or cardboard over the cup.
4. Poke the pencils through the cover and into the water, making sure they don't touch the bottom.
5. Making sure the pencils don't touch, place your battery atop the pencils, so that each tip contacts one of the terminals of the battery.
6. Watch as tiny bubbles of hydrogen and oxygen gas are produced within the water—this process is called electrolysis!
7. If you don't see gas, you may need to make the water more conductive by adding some salt. Or, perhaps your 9-volt battery is out of juice.

You've learned about the chemistry behind all sorts of electric technologies. Now it's time to see that science in action!

Try this next!

How could you measure the different gases produced in electrolysis? Maybe you could switch around the experiment somewhat—instead of pencils, you could use pushpins and stick them in the bottom of a plastic cup. Then, you could put a narrow glass or test tube over each pushpin, so that the bubbles of gas produced float up and collect in the tubes. Which test tube do you think would fill up first: hydrogen or oxygen?

QUESTION TIME!

What chemical process covered in this book is most similar to this experiment? Why do you think hydrogen and oxygen gas are produced when the electric current runs into the water? Can you think of any cool uses for this technology?

Index

A
aldehydes, 43
anodes, 16-17, 20-22, 25, 41
Arfvedson, Johann, 18
atomic bonds, 7, 10-11, 16, 28-29, 32-33, 41
atoms, 6-14, 16, 18, 20, 22, 28-30, 32-33, 41

B
batteries, 14-25, 29, 40, 44
Berzelius, Jöns, 30
bipolar disorder, 19
boron, 33
buckyballs, 11

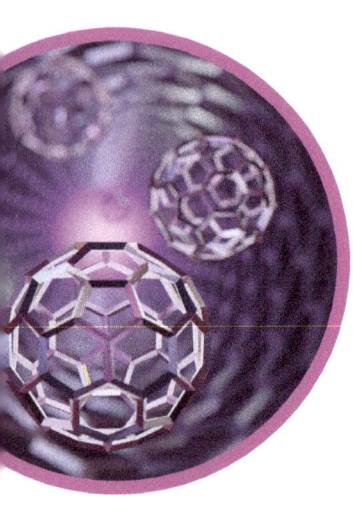

C
cadmium sulfide, 13
carbon, 10-11, 16, 20-22, 31
carbon nanotubes, 10-11
Carborundum, 31
cathodes, 16-17, 20-22, 25, 41
chemical reactions, 16, 18-19, 21, 40, 43
climate change, 34-35, 37, 39, 43
copper, 15, 21, 27-28
crust, of Earth, 31
crystals, 8, 12-13, 27-30, 32-33, 38-39

D
doping (chemical process), 32-33, 36-37

E
electric current, 10, 14, 16, 20-22, 27, 29, 36-37, 45
electrolytes, 15-16, 20-23, 25
electrolysis, 44-45
electron beam lithography, 9
electrons, 6-7, 14, 16, 18, 20-21, 27-29, 32-33, 36-37, 41
environmental science (career), 43

G
germanium, 27
glass, 19, 27-28, 30, 36, 38
greenhouse gases, 34, 41

H
hydrogen, 7, 19, 35, 40-41, 44-45
hydroxide, 25

I
Industrial Revolution, 35
ions, 20-22
iron, 15, 25

L
light-emitting diodes (LED's), 27
lithium, 15, 17-23

M
manganese dioxide, 17
molecules, 7, 9-10, 12-13, 16, 25, 28, 41-42

N
nanotechnology, 8-11
National Aeronautics and Space Administration (NASA), 25
neutrons, 6, 29

O
oxidation, 16
oxygen, 7, 30-31, 38, 40-41, 44-45

P
perovskite, 34, 38-39
phosphorus, 33
photocatalysis, 35, 41
photovoltaic effect, 37
physical chemistry (career), 13
plastics, 9, 35, 42-43
pollution, 34-35, 42-43
polymers, 42
primary batteries, 17
protons, 6, 18, 28-29
pyrolysis, 43

Q
quantum dots, 12-13
quartz, 30

R
recycling, 35, 42-43
rust, 24-25

S
secondary batteries, 17
semiconductors, 12-13, 26-34, 36-37, 41
silicates, 30-31
silicon, 22, 26-34, 38
silicon dioxide, 30
silicones, 31
solar energy, 24, 26, 31, 34, 36-40
solid-state batteries, 22-23

T
transistors, 31, 37

U
ultraviolet light, 12

W
water, 7, 19, 35, 40-41, 44-45

Z
zinc, 16-17

Glossary

atom (AT uhm)—an incredibly tiny particle that makes up all things

battery (BAT uhr ee)—a device that stores energy as chemical energy and releases it as electric energy

bond (bond)—the attraction, due to electrons, that holds atoms together

carbon (KAHR buhn)—a very common chemical element which occurs in combination with other elements in all plants and animals

crystal (KRIHS tuhl)—a solid that is composed of atoms arranged in an orderly pattern

current (KUR uhnt)—the movement or flow of electric charges, such as electrons

electron (ih LEHK tron)—a negatively charged particle that is smaller than the atom

ion (EYE uhn)—an atom or molecule that has an electric charge, often positive

lithium (LIHTH ee uhm)—soft, silvery-white metallic element, the lightest known metal

molecule (MOL uh kyool)—a group of joined atoms

reaction (ree AK shuhn)—a process by which one or more substances are converted into one or more different substances

semiconductor (SEHM ee kuhn DUHK tuhr)—a material that conducts electric current better than an insulator like glass, but not as well as a conductor like copper

silicon (SIHL uh kuhn)—a hard, dark gray metalloid element that has a shiny luster

water (WAWT uhr)—a very important molecule made of two hydrogen atoms and one oxygen atom

www.ingramcontent.com/pod-product-compliance
Lightning Source LLC
Chambersburg PA
CBHW061250170426
43191CB00041B/2408